Reproducible Activities

Daily Warmups

Math Problems & Puzzles

Grade 5

D1709785

Instructional Fair
An imprint of Carson-Dellosa Publishing LLC
Greensboro, North Carolina

Instructional Fair
An imprint of Carson-Dellosa Publishing LLC
P.O. Box 35665
Greensboro, NC 27425 USA

Printed in the USA • All rights reserved.   ISBN 0-7424-1795-6

Table of Contents

NCTM Standards	Problem Number
Number and Operations	4, 5, 9, 12, 15, 19, 24, 26, 31, 34, 35, 37, 40, 42, 43, 48, 50, 54, 56, 57, 60, 61, 68, 70, 71, 73, 75, 80, 81, 83, 86, 87, 96, 98, 99, 103, 106, 110, 112, 116, 119, 122, 123, 130, 135, 144, 149, 157, 160, 162, 164, 165, 167, 170, 172, 173, 181, 184, 185, 187, 190, 192, 193, 196, 197, 199, 202, 204, 206, 208, 209, 212, 213, 216, 217, 219, 222, 224, 225, 227, 230, 231, 234
Algebra	1, 13, 16, 21, 27, 32, 39, 44, 46, 47, 52, 55, 63, 65, 67, 69, 78, 79, 85, 88, 90, 92, 94, 109, 114, 115, 117, 120, 121, 124, 126, 127, 131, 133, 138, 140, 142, 143, 146, 148, 153, 155, 158, 161, 163, 166, 171, 176, 179, 183, 186, 188, 189, 194, 205, 207, 215, 218, 221, 223, 226, 228, 229, 233
Geometry	6, 8, 11, 14, 30, 36, 45, 62, 66, 74, 76, 82, 93, 95, 97, 108, 125, 129, 145, 156, 159, 168, 177, 180, 214
Measurement	2, 17, 22, 29, 49, 72, 84, 100, 101, 113, 118, 128, 132, 141, 169, 174, 175, 182, 191, 195, 198, 200, 210, 220
Data Analysis and Probability	3, 10, 18, 20, 23, 25, 38, 41, 51, 53, 58, 59, 64, 89, 91, 102, 104, 105, 107, 137, 150, 152, 178, 203, 232
Problem Solving	7, 28, 33, 77, 111, 134, 136, 139, 147, 151, 154, 201, 211

Introduction

This book is one in a series of books from grade K through grade 8. Each book provides a wide variety of challenging and engaging grade-appropriate problems and puzzles from all areas of the math curriculum. Each book contains 234 problems and puzzles, one for each day of the school year plus more. All are keyed to the appropriate National Council of Teachers of Mathematics (NCTM) standards, and many are designed for hands-on problem solving with common classroom manipulatives. Some call for the use of standard six-sided dice. A die pattern is provided on page 5 for your convenience. Two copies of a dot array are also included. Other problems call for colored cubes, dice, and calculators. However, most problems require only paper and pencil and a little brainpower. Please note that many measurement activities use only either customary or metric units. These activities are intended to give practice with the measurement noted.

Each page contains two problems or puzzles. The problems are reproducible and are suitable to use with an overhead projector. Most offer ample space for problem solving. The problems and puzzles in this book are designed to be solved within 15 minutes, but most will take 5 minutes or less. These problems are great for use as early-morning warmups or for the beginning of math class and can be used independently or in groups. You can also assign problems as homework or as a math lab activity. Another idea is to use these problems in class competitions. Which group or individual will be the first to solve the problem?

Work through a few problems before your students begin to work independently or in groups. As you do so, it is important to model a problem-solving process. Stress that many problems have multiple solutions. Then, watch as your students grow and develop their own problem-solving strategies and gain a new appreciation for math.

Dot Arrays/Die Pattern

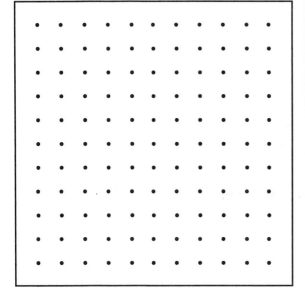
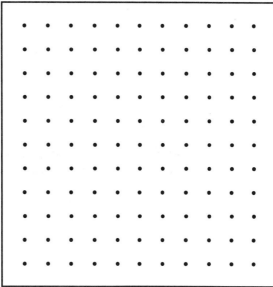

Pattern for Regul

1

Algebra

The paramecium is a single-celled organism too small to see without a microscope. It divides into 2 new organisms about once a day. At this rate, how many paramecia will exist after 14 days if the original paramecium divided on day 1 and all of the future generations survive? Will it take more than a month to reach 1,000,000 paramecia? Estimate and then confirm your estimate by determining the exact number of days it would take to reach 1,000,000 paramecia. 5,00,000 days

2

M

Restaura

the
m—or so they
. Measure from
yd. away. Follow
s 100 yd.

Data Analysis and Probability

This pie chart shows how Daniela spent the $40.00 she earned from baby-sitting during August. Use the pie chart to estimate how much money she spent on each category.

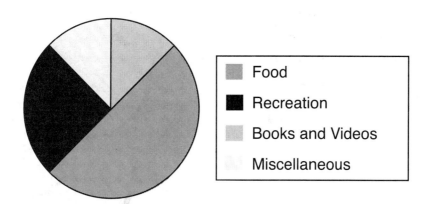

- Food
- Recreation
- Books and Videos
- Miscellaneous

Number and Operations

Cullum and Declan bought an old aquarium at a garage sale for $6.00. Then they sent away for a shipment of tadpoles to sell. They bought 100 tadpoles at $0.05 each. Unfortunately, they didn't sell a single tadpole—even though all of them lived. They had croaking frogs instead of cute little tadpoles. When the neighbors began to complain, Cullum's parents made the boys take their frogs to the Humane Society. The Humane Society take the frogs only if the boys agreed to pay the society $0.15 a frog. How much did this business deal end up costing the boys? First estimate your answer. Then use a calculator to find the exact figures.

Number and Operations

Kwan was arranging the CDs for the rummage sale. He had 5 different groups. He put $\frac{1}{8}$ of the CDs in the jazz section, $\frac{1}{4}$ in the rap section, $\frac{3}{8}$ in the rock section, and $\frac{3}{16}$ in the pop section. He put $\frac{1}{16}$ in the classical section.

There are 3 CDs in the classical section. How many CDs did Kwan arrange altogether?

Geometry

Read the shape riddle and draw the answer.

I have 4 sides.
All 4 sides are the same length.
None of the sides are perpendicular.
What am I?

Problem Solving

The victims of 3 robbers could tell police only 3 things: the robbers were either men or women, they were very ugly, 1 had red hair, 1 had black hair, and 1 had blonde hair. The police got lucky. They spotted the robbers inside a store and ordered them to come out with their hands up. Assuming that the robbers left the store one at a time, list all of the possible orders in which they might have exited, using their hair color to identify them.

Geometry

How many rectangles can you find in this picture?

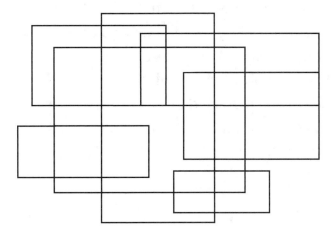

Number and Operations

Use 3 of these 4 fractions to make true equations in each case below. $\frac{1}{6}$ $\frac{1}{4}$ $\frac{1}{3}$ $\frac{1}{2}$

 a   _____ + _____ + _____ = 1

 b   _____ + _____ + _____ = $1\frac{1}{12}$

 c   _____ + _____ − _____ = $\frac{5}{12}$

 d   _____ + _____ − _____ = $\frac{7}{12}$

e   _____ − _____ + _____ = $\frac{2}{3}$

Data Analysis and Probability

Radio station WEAR is sponsoring the Great Cash Drop. At noon, the WEAR helicopter will fly over the downtown area, dropping 1,000 one-dollar bills, 500 five-dollar bills, and 100 ten-dollar bills. If you managed to pick up 1 bill, what are the odds that you would have $10.00?

Geometry

Pieter and Rafael built a bike ramp from 20 sheets of 4 ft. x 8 ft. plywood and propped it up on one end with some bricks. The finished ramp is rectangular. Show 3 ways they might have arranged the wood and give the measurements for each side. Assuming that they used every sheet of plywood, what is the total area of the ramp regardless of its shape?

Number and Operations

David has been saving his allowance and working around the neighborhood for weeks. He wants to earn enough money to buy the latest skater video game. He earns $15.00 a month mowing his neighbor's lawn. His mom paid him $5.50 for helping at the garage sale. His dad gave him $5.75 for washing the car. Miss Burke paid him $12.00 for walking her dog every day after school. He has saved $13.75 from his allowance. The cost of the game is $49.99 plus 8% sales tax. How much more money does he need to earn before he can buy the game?

Algebra

In a single-elimination soccer tournament with 16 teams, how many games will have to be played to determine the winning team?

Geometry

A building casts a shadow that is 7.5 ft. long. A person standing next to the building casts a shadow that is 3 ft. long. If the person is 5 ft. tall, how tall is the building? (**HINT:** the sides of similar triangles are in proportion.)

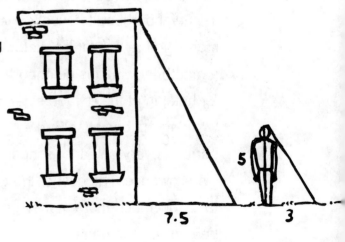

5

7.5   3

Number and Operations

Ms. Hale's class is the official product tester for a new children's toy, Giggly Goop. The manufacturer claims the goop will double in weight after warming for an hour in the sun. Each student was given 5 oz. of the stuff in a small container. One of the students went inside for lunch and forgot her goop. She left it outside for 3 hours. While she was gone, the goop increased in weight by 1,000% during the first hour, doubled that weight in the second hour, and in the third hour, it increased yet another 2,000%. How much did the growing goop weigh by the time the student came back to get it? Round your answer to the nearest whole number and express it in pounds.

Algebra

Find the pattern and fill in the missing numbers.

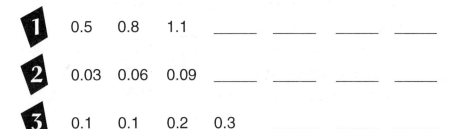

1   0.5   0.8   1.1   _____   _____   _____   _____

2   0.03   0.06   0.09   _____   _____   _____   _____

3   0.1   0.1   0.2   0.3   _____   _____   _____

Measurement

If a room measuring 12 ft. x 15 ft. is to be covered with carpeting that costs $10.00 per square yard, how much will the carpeting cost for the entire room?

Data Analysis and Probability

Draw a tree diagram to show each possible outcome from the description below.

Each high school student must sign up for 1 language class and 1 music class. The language choices are French, Spanish, German, or Latin. The music choices are choir, symphony, or band.

Number and Operations

19

Saad and Sato have been working on a computer project and want to protect their work. They decide to use the sum of all of the prime numbers between 0 and 50 as the password. What is their password?

Data Analysis and Probability

20

Use the information to complete the pie graph.
Trash collected on Earth Day:

paper	50%
aluminum cans	15%
plastic	15%
rubber	10%
glass	10%

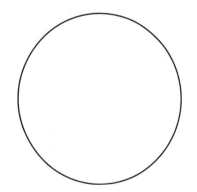

Algebra

The figure below is made up of 16 toothpicks of equal length. Use 8 more toothpicks to divide the area into 4 equal and similar-shaped areas without moving any of the existing toothpicks. Use real toothpicks to help you.

Measurement

Grandma is crocheting a striped afghan. It will have 16 stripes in all, using 3 colors following this pattern: green, yellow, blue, green, yellow, blue, etc. If each stripe uses 2 oz. of yarn, how many ounces of each color yarn will Grandma need?

Data Analysis and Probability

23

Poor Chris has sneezed at least 50 times every day for 10 days out of the last 2 weeks. What is the ratio of sneeze-free days to sneeze-filled days? If this pattern continues, how many days will he sneeze in 3 weeks?

Number and Operations

24

Kylie wants to buy her sister's mountain bike for $50.00, so she has taken on several jobs. The chart below shows the jobs she has done in the past 2 weeks, and her rate of pay for each.

Job	Rate	Hours Worked
Raking Mrs. Sung's lawn	$2.75 per hour	6
Baby-sitting the Jaffa twins	$1.85 per hour per twin, per hour	5
Grocery shopping for Mr. Johnson	$0.95 per hour, plus a 10% tip of the $120.00 bill	2

Estimate her total earnings. Do you think she'll have enough to buy the bicycle? Now figure her exact earnings. Use a calculator to check your answers.

Data Analysis and Probability

The fifth grade class is having a jump-a-thon to see how many times each person can jump rope without missing. The results are below.

Gary—   25

John—   34

Bruce—   41

Lori—   43

Teather—   24

Stephanie—36

Melissa—   31

Jannette—   40

Carol—   26

Ron—   24

Teri—   26

Record the jump-a-thon scores on a line plot.

Number and Operations

Marissa collects coupons that are worth $\frac{1}{10}$ of a cent. After she spent half of her coupons on a coin purse, she still had 7,508 coupons. What was the value of her coupons before the purchase? Round your answer to the nearest tenth of a cent.

Algebra

Read the information below. Three answers are given. Write an appropriate question for each answer. The seventh grade class is planning a field trip. The class of 145 students and 5 chaperones plan to travel by bus. Each bus can transport 35 people.

 a If the answer is 4, what is the question?

 b If the answer is 5, what is the question?

 c If the answer is 10, what is the question?

Problem Solving

You have agreed to be home at noon. There is just one problem—the hands on your watch move only 30 minutes every hour. You set it to the proper time at 8:00 A.M. Currently your watch reads 10:30 A.M., but it stopped exactly 2 hours ago when you accidentally hit it against the wall while riding your bike. What time is it now?

Measurement

The tallest mountain in the world is not Mt. Everest . . . it is the entire island of Hawaii. Hawaii's tallest peak is Mauna Kea, which rises 13,784 ft. above sea level. The base of the mountain reaches down 18,000 ft. below sea level. If you are planning to climb the entire mountain, you'd better take along your deep-sea diving equipment. Calculate what percentage of your climb will actually be underwater.

Geometry

There are 47 triangles in this figure.
How many are right triangles?
How many are equilateral triangles?
What other types of triangles can
you find?

Number and Operations

Anastasia and Molly ate a pizza. There are 8 pieces in the pizza. Anastasia ate more than $\frac{1}{2}$ but less than $\frac{2}{3}$. Molly ate the rest of the pizza. How many eighths of the pizza did each of them eat?

Anastasia ate _____ .

Molly ate _____ .

Algebra

The Davis family is planning a long journey of 3,600 mi. They plan to drive 200 mi. the first day, 400 mi. the second day, and 600 mi. the third day. Then they will repeat the 3-day pattern until their journey is over. For how many days will the Davises be traveling?

Problem Solving

Four friends are sitting at a table talking about sports. They each like a different sport: volleyball, soccer, hockey, and swimming. Read the clues and find where each friend is sitting at the table and which sport she likes. Note: each person is facing the table.

- Alani is sitting between a girl who plays soccer and the swimmer.
- Kenya is across the table from the girl who plays hockey.
- Julieta is to the left of the girl who plays hockey.
- The soccer player is sitting across from Teresa.

Number and Operations

How many 2-digit whole numbers are there? Explain how you found your answer.

Number and Operations

Helen's Health Foods is giving away this recipe for punch. However, someone forgot to convert a few fractions in this recipe to their lowest terms. Convert each fraction to lowest terms using common denominators. How many cups of nuts and juice are used in the recipe altogether?

> **Unfiltered Mixed Nut Punch**
>
> $4 \frac{6}{5}$ cups orange juice
>
> $5 \frac{2}{3}$ cups apple juice
>
> $1 \frac{15}{15}$ cups chopped walnuts
>
> $\frac{5}{6}$ cup blanched almonds
>
> Place in a blender on high for 15 minutes.
>
> Enjoy!

Geometry

Lincoln Middle School has entered a team in Marathon of the Mind, a creative problem-solving competition. The team has constructed a triangular-shaped car that runs on solar energy. They must construct a trailer to transport the car to the competition. Find the area of the trailer floor if the car, which is 5 ft. wide (at its widest point) and 9 ft. long, fills the trailer completely. Now draw a diagram of the car inside the trailer.

Numbers and Operations

This number has 4 places to the right of the decimal point. It has 2 hundreds, 3 ten thousandths, and 1 tenth. It is between 240 and 242. The thousandths place is 1 less than the ten thousandths and less than the hundredths. What are 6 numbers that match this data?

Data Analysis and Probability

Two hundred people were asked whether they preferred regular, diet, or classic Fruit Fiz soda. Responses showed that 10% preferred diet and 20% preferred regular. How many people chose classic?

Algebra

The following Venn diagram has been completed except for the labels. Look at the numbers in each region. Write an appropriate label in each box.

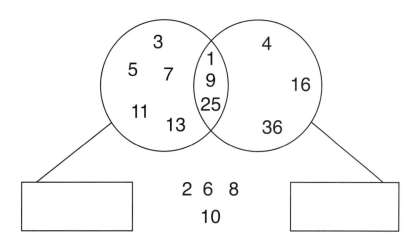

Number and Operations

Insert the operations symbols <, >, and = to make this a true sentence.

2.7   27 $\frac{3}{4}$ $\frac{6}{8}$ 68

Data Analysis and Probability

Use a pair of dice.

Begin with 50 points and your dice. Roll the dice. Each time the sum of the dots on the dice is an even number, you double your score; each time the sum is an odd number, you lose half your score. If you happen to roll doubles (each die showing the same number), you triple your score. How many points do you have at the end of 10 rolls of the dice? Also, is it ever possible to roll doubles and have the sum of the dice be an odd number?

Number and Operations

Each even number shown in the triangles is the sum of 2 prime numbers. Write the 2 primes that total each even number in the triangles below.

Example:

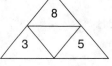

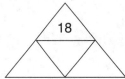   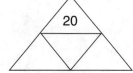   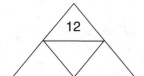

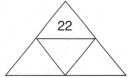   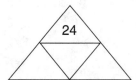

Number and Operations

43

Melissa shared her birthday cake with 5 friends. She and her friends each had $\frac{1}{8}$ of the cake. Her brother ate $\frac{1}{16}$ of the cake. Her dog ate the rest. What part of the cake did her dog eat? Name the fraction and shade the cake to show it.

Algebra

44

A mother is 49 years old, and her daughter is 19. How many years ago was the mother 3 times as old as her daughter?

Geometry

It's a fact: pot-bellied pigs have become a popular pet to have. Can you put each of these pigs in its own pen by drawing just 2 four-sided figures? Draw your solution.

Algebra

Use the following clues and a hundreds chart to find the mystery number or numbers.

- The number is a prime number between 0 and 50.
- The number is odd.
- It is not a multiple of 5.
- The sum of the 2 digits is less than 7.
- The number is not a palindrome.

Algebra

Mom believes that the washing machine has a mind of its own. Every time she washes socks, the washing machine seems to be using its own rules about how many socks go in the washing machine and how many socks come out. Look at the graphs and find the algebraic rule Mom thinks the machine is using each laundry day.

Saturday Rule:

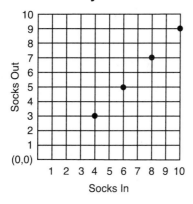

Wednesday Rule:

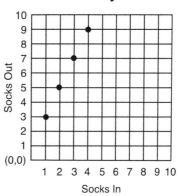

Number and Operations

And now . . . a mystery number!

I am the difference between the 2 largest prime numbers less than 100. The Greeks named my geometric shape octagonal. I am the number 2 to the third power.

What am I?

Measurement

Welcome to Boomville! So many people are moving into Boomville that the Boomville Sign Shop needs to make new street signs. A standard street sign is 30 in. high and 30 in. wide. How many new street signs can be cut from a 50-ft. x 100-ft. sheet of steel?

Number and Operations

If even numbers are zucchini and odd numbers are radishes, . . .

 what is a radish multiplied by a radish?

 what is a zucchini multiplied by a zucchini?

 what is a radish multiplied by a zucchini?

Data Analysis and Probability

The line graph shows concert attendance over several years. Which description below matches the data displayed in the line graph?

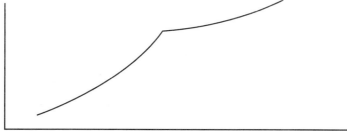

a   Attendance was high the first year but fell the last year.

b   Attendance was low the first year. Then it went up and stayed up.

c   Attendance was low the first year. It went up, but it fell the last year.

Algebra

The sum of 2 numbers is 24.

Their product is 80.

What are the 2 numbers?

Data Analysis and Probability

Use colored cubes or tiles and a paper or plastic bag.

Yaron is late for school . . . again. Without looking he reaches into his sock drawer. In the drawer are 8 red socks and 9 green socks. What is the probability that he will pull out a green sock and then another green sock?

Record the probability on a sheet of paper that will serve as your data recorder for this activity. Then, place 8 red and 9 green cubes in a bag. Try pulling out a pair of cubes. If you make a color match, record it, replace the cubes, and try again. If you don't, leave the 2 cubes out of the bag and try again. What is the probability of pulling out a matching pair now? Record the probability and then test to see how many times you have to try before getting a matching pair.

Number and Operations

A brother and sister each have the same amount of money. How much of her money should the sister give her brother so that he has $10.00 more than she has?

Algebra

As an April Fool's Day trick, Ruth and John decided to spread the rumor that there would be no school on April first. On the first day they told 6 friends. On the second day 12 more friends were told. On the third day 24 more students were told. By getting more and more people involved, they were able to spread the rumor to twice as many students each day as had been told the day before. If there are 320 people in the school, how long will it take to spread the rumor to everyone?

Number and Operations

If day 1 of a 30-day cruise is on a Wednesday, what day of the week would be day 30?

Number and Operations

How many 2-digit whole numbers contain a least one 7?

Data Analysis and Probability

This pie graph shows the results of a survey of 200 sixth graders. They were asked to name their favorite type of music. Read the clues to figure out what section of the pie graph represents each kind of music. Label each section.

 a Almost $\frac{1}{2}$ of the students chose rock and roll.

 b Almost $\frac{1}{4}$ of the students chose country.

 c About $\frac{1}{8}$ of the students chose jazz, and about $\frac{1}{8}$ chose new age.

 d Less than $\frac{1}{8}$ of the students chose classical.

Data Analysis and Probability

59

Create a pie graph that shows how the campers at Brisburn Summer Community Activities Camp spent their time. Group the activities below into the following categories and convert the total time spent in each activity as a percentage of the day: eating, sports, bus travel, math/reading/science, community clean up, and museums.

7:30	breakfast	12:30	community clean up
8:00	math	1:30	visit museums
9:00	science	2:30	bus travel
10:00	snack	3:00	swimming
10:15	sports	4:15	snack
11:30	lunch	4:30	reading
12:00	bus travel	5:30	end of day

Number and Operations

60

Tao's older sister is buying an old Triumph sports car. She had $825.00 in her savings account, and the car will cost $1\frac{2}{3}$ that amount. Does she have to borrow money to pay the full price for the car? If so, how much will she have to borrow? If not, how much will she have left over?

Number and Operations

An antique dealer bought a silver spoon for $5.00 and sold it for $6.00. He then bought the same spoon back for $7.00 and sold it for $8.00. How much profit did the dealer make in all?

Geometry

The 3 angles of a triangle equal 180°. You can use this fact to find the sum of all the angles in a polygon. Draw diagonal lines in the polygon below to break it into triangles. Then calculate the sum of the angles in the polygon. Look at the example for help.

Example:

3 triangles x 180°/triangle = 540°

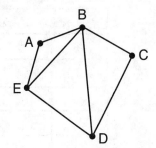

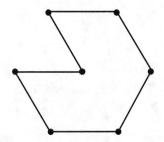

Algebra

Neal is an insect collector who has been losing a lot of insects lately. His favorite insect, a common housefly with green wings, disappeared last week—along with several other insects. He began his collection with 48 insects. At the beginning of each week he adds 6 more, but when he opens the lid once each week, 12 insects escape. Create a line graph that shows how many insects Neal will have at the beginning of weeks 1 through 5. How many weeks will it take before Neal has no insects left in his collection?

Data Analysis and Probability

Chandra and her sister have entered the mountaineering club's cross-country foot race. The starting line is broken down into 5 groups, with each group made up of runners approximately the same age and same ability. Complete the group chart below by filling in numbers so that every row and every column equals 75 runners. Some of the group numbers have been filled in for you.

	Ability Levels				
	a	b	c	d	e
8–10	8	14	28	9	16
11–13	8	13			
14–16	20		17		
17–19	22			12	
20–22	17				25

Algebra

Becky and her 7 closest friends decided that they need to keep in better touch. Once a week they will each speak to everyone else in the group on the phone. How many phone calls will be made each week in all? How many phone calls would be made if there were 20 people in Becky's group of friends?

Geometry

Look at this figure. Can you draw an exact replica of it without lifting your pencil from the paper and without going over the same part twice?

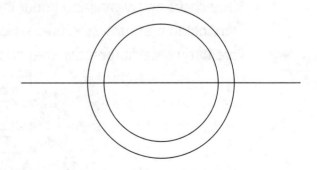

Algebra

Emma's class is sponsoring Science Night for parents. For her demonstration, Emma is growing yeast buds in a beaker. She places 3 times as many milliliters of water in the beaker as she does of yeast. The combined solution in the beaker measures 9 mL. Figure out the amounts of yeast and water she used.

Number and Operations

The numbers 1–9 fit in the puzzle below.
Use the clues to put each number where it belongs.

Each corner is an even number.
The middle row contains 3 odd numbers.
The sum of each row and column is odd.
The sum of the numbers in the middle row is 3 times the sum of the top row.
The numbers in the third column are factors of 56.
The product of the numbers in the bottom row is the same as 12 x 12.

Algebra

If A = 1, B = 2, C = 3, D = 4. etc., what are the sums of these words?

 a   dab

 b   baby

 c   cabbage

Number and Operations

Adolfo has 50 blue and white marbles. Thirty-five of them are blue. What percentage of Adolfo's marbles are white?

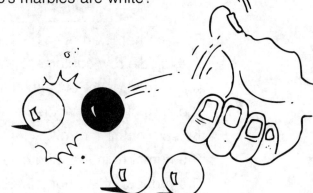

Number and Operations

Karem had such a large paper route that he needed help getting all of the 486 papers delivered on time. He divided the route into thirds, keeping $\frac{1}{3}$ for himself and dividing the remaining route evenly among 6 carriers. How many papers did he personally deliver? How many did each of the other carriers deliver? Draw a diagram to show how the route was divided.

Measurement

Draw 6 different ways to divide the area of a square in half. Shade in one-half of each square below.

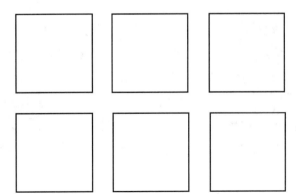

Number and Operations

Did you know that you can figure out if a large number is divisible by 8 without actually having to divide the whole thing first? To do this, look first at the hundreds, tens, and ones digits. Is this number divisible by 8? For example, 145,120 is divisible by 8 since 120 divided by 8 equals 15. Now determine which of the numbers below are divisible by 8. Then list 4 additional numbers (of at least 6 digits) that are divisible by 8.

 a   3,576,808

 b   4,465,168

 c   48

 d   965,354,960

Geometry

The school spirit committee wants to create giant paper disks for each member of the soccer team to break through at the start of the state finals. Each paper disk will be painted with a picture of the school's mascot. Find the total area of paper they will need if there are 18 players on the soccer team and each disk will have a radius of 4 ft. Round your answer to the nearest tenth of a foot. If they use 1 gallon of paint for every 12 sq. ft. of paper, how many gallons of paint will they need?

Number and Operations

Here is an example of a factor tree.

54
9 x 6
3 x 3 3 x 2

Create a factor tree for each of the following numbers:

 49   212   88

Geometry

The old hickory tree in front of the courthouse was damaged in a windstorm. It now stands at an angle of 84° to the ground. The city's chief forester believes that the tree will fall completely over when it reaches an angle of 48°. He wants to attach a cable to the tree to hold it in place, but it will take 14 days for the cable to arrive. If the angle of the tree to the ground increases by 3° every 12 hours, is there enough time for the cable to arrive? Prove your answer.

Problem Solving

The fifth grade is putting on a play for Kinder Courtyard Preschool. M.J., the class president, agreed to help Mr. Fine walk his class from the classroom to the gymnasium. If there were at least 3 kindergarteners, in front of a fifth grader, 3 kindergarteners behind a fifth grader, what is the smallest possible number of students in M.J.'s line?

Algebra

Oscar and Olga printed 50 flyers for next week's Sports Day. They have 3 different kinds of stickers to put on the flyers. They put a soccer sticker on each flyer. They put a baseball sticker on every fourth flyer. They put a basketball sticker on every fifth flyer. How many flyers have all 3 kinds of stickers on them?

Algebra

Alex's older sister Natasha bought a new computer. Unfortunately, the computer came with a virus on the 200-gigabyte hard drive. The virus destroys 25% of the data remaining on the drive each day. If the drive was completely full when she first bought it, how many gigabytes of data will Natasha have on the drive at the end of 10 days, assuming she had 200 gigabytes at the end of the first day? Round your answer to the nearest tenth.

Number and Operations

The following equations, when completed from left to right, all equal 8. Insert the proper operation signs (+, −, x, ÷) to complete each equation. You may not use the same sequence of operations in more than one equation. Will the sequences you used work if you substitute another number for all the 8s? Try it to find out.

```
8 8 8 8 8 = 8
8 8 8 8 8 = 8
8 8 8 8 8 = 8
8 8 8 8 8 = 8
8 8 8 8 8 = 8
```

Number and Operations

Estimate how much money the Schneider family spends on peanut butter and jelly sandwiches for 1 year. The Schneiders buy 2 loaves of bread per week at an average cost of $1.50 per loaf. They buy 3 jars of peanut butter per month at a cost of $3.00 per jar. They buy 2 jars of jelly per month at a cost of $2.00 per jar. What is the family's yearly expense for the sandwiches?

Geometry

Draw as many straight lines as listed to divide the triangle below into the shapes listed.

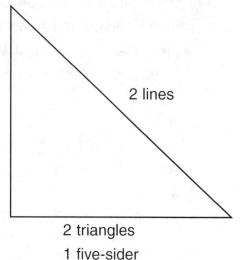

2 lines

2 triangles

1 five-sider

Number and Operations

A library charges a circulation fee of $1.00 per video, $0.50 per CD, and $0.25 per cassette. Tyrone wants to check out 5 CDs and 6 cassettes. How much money will he need?

Measurement

A picture frame's outer dimensions are 20 in. x 12 in. If the frame mat is 1 in. wide all the way around, what is the area of the picture inside the frame?

Algebra

The roller coaster at the theme park has 6 steep hills and 8 loops. The first hill has a vertical drop of 300 ft. The second has a drop of 275 ft. The third has a drop of 325 ft. The fourth drops 300 ft. again. If the change in vertical drops is a repeating pattern, what will the drops for the next 2 hills be?

Number and Operations

Lisa's grandmother enjoys talking in the park with her 2 good friends. When a storm destroyed the park bench they sit on, as well as the nearby flower garden, Lisa decided to start a fund-raising campaign to get them repaired. The city council agreed to help and gave Lisa an amount of money equal to 50 times the greatest common divisor of the $40.00 needed for the plants, the $76.00 for the grass, and the $112.00 for the benches. The local chamber of commerce donated 10% of the amount given by the city council, and the staff at the senior center contributed 80% of the amount donated by the local chamber of commerce. How much money does Lisa have now? How much must she still collect to get the job done?

0-7424-1795-6 *Daily Warmups*

Number and Operations

87

Working on commission from sales can be very hard work. For example, suppose you sell a set of books for $200.00. If your boss has agreed to pay you a 5% commission, you earn $10.00 for your work and the company gets $190.00. Use this information to fill in the chart. Use a calculator for help.

Name	Commission Rate	Net Sales ($)	Total Commission
Jason	5%	128.00	
Gen	8%		24.16
Juan		51.00	6.12
Devon	15%		31.80
Gretchen	9%	468.00	

Algebra

Imagine that you suddenly doubled your height every day for a week, beginning on Sunday. How tall would you be on the following Saturday?

49

49

Data Analysis and Probability

Use play money.

What is the probability of flipping 2 coins and getting 2 heads? What is the probability of getting 2 tails? What is the probability of getting 1 head and 1 tail? Explain how it is possible to have a better chance at getting 1 head and 1 tail, and then draw all of the possible combinations when you flip 2 coins.

Algebra

Look at the set of numbers below. They are not in any particular order. Find something they have in common. Write a rule to go with the set. List 5 more numbers that could be part of the set.

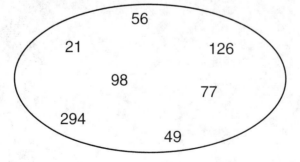

56

21   126

98

77

294

49

Rule:

Five other numbers:

Data Analysis and Probability

Which of these 3 events has the lowest probability?

a rolling a number lower than 4 on a die

b rolling a number higher than 4 on a die

c rolling an odd number on a die

Algebra

Together a cat and dog weigh 20 lb. The dog weighs 3 times as much as the cat. How much does each animal weigh?

Geometry

Hisako is constructing a model city of the future. She plans to construct only pyramid-shaped buildings. Fill in the chart below, using the formula: Area = $\frac{\text{base} \times \text{height}}{2}$ to help you.

Using the measurements on the chart, what will be the total surface area of each building?

Type of Pyramid	Each Edge of Base (in.)	Height of Face (in.)	Area of Each Face (sq. in.)	Number of Faces	Total Surface Area of Faces (sq. in.)
triangular	4"	3"			
square	4"	4"			
hexagonal	4"	6"			

Algebra

This mystery number is not divisible by 3.

Its tens digit is less than its ones digit.

One of its digits is odd, the other is even.

It is not a multiple of 2.

The sum of its digits is more than 10.

It is a square number.

The mystery number is _____ .

Geometry

Shade triangles in each shape below to make three different four-sided shapes.

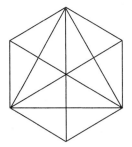 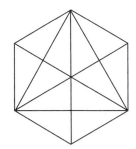 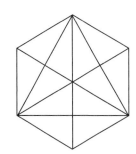

Number and Operations

Out of the entire population of 360 students at Marne Elementary School, 80 students do not ride the bus. What percentage of the students ride the bus?

Geometry

Draw 2 lines across the hexagon to divide it into the shapes listed.

2 triangles
1 rectangle

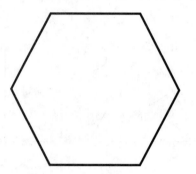

Number and Operations

As part of their personal finance class, Mr. Richardson's students were supposed to track a particular stock, watching its performance. Aleen and Charissa decided to track 100 shares of stock from ToyTime, Inc., which cost $1.25 per share. The first week, the stock decreased in value by 12%. The second week it increased by 20%. The third week the stock decreased in value by 60%. Create a line graph that shows the changes in the value of ToyTime stock over the 3 weeks. Use a calculator to help you with percents. Make up values for weeks 4, 5, and 6.

0-7424-1795-6 *Daily Warmups*

Number and Operations

Marielle, Jacob, and Vanda all baby-sit for the Davis twins, also known as the Gruesome Twosome. The twins are so difficult to manage that everyone who baby-sits for them has

decided to raise their prices by 25%. Marielle was charging $2.50 an hour, Jacob was charging $2.25, and Vanda was charging $2.75. Estimate the increase in each of the salaries. Then use a calculator to find the exact answer. Round each raise to the nearest cent.

Measurement

The fifth grade has agreed to help the kindergarten construct a life-size Tyrannosaurus rex on the side of the school building. The students know from their studies of dinosaurs that the average T-Rex stood 18 ft. high and was 50 ft. long. They plan to construct the single-dimension model out of green plastic trash bags. If each trash bag measures 1 ft. wide and $2\frac{1}{2}$ ft. long, how many bags will they need to make sure they have enough for an average-sized model T-Rex?

Measurement

The Blues are a very tall family. Mrs. Blue is 70 in. tall, which is 85% of Mr. Blue's height and 4 in. shorter than Andy. The height of Andy's twin brother Vandy is the average of Andy and Mrs. Blue's heights. How tall is each of the Blues (to the nearest inch)? Express each height as a combination of feet and inches.

Data Analysis and Probability

Carla wants a raise in her allowance, without having additional chores. In an effort to convince her parents that her allowance was below average, she surveyed her friends and presented the list to her parents. If her parents agree to pay her the average, what should Carla's allowance be?

Name	Allowance
Jolene	$8.00
Carla	$7.00
Donna	$11.00
Janelle	$16.00
Analisa	$10.00
Marissa	$9.00
Renee	$15.00
Caroline	$12.00

Number and Operations

What numeral does the Roman numeral MCMLXXVI represent?

Data Analysis and Probability

A facial glyph is a graph that tells about a person. Use the key below to make a facial glyph that will tell others about you, your family, your likes, and how you spend your time.

EYES Favorite Subject	Reading ô ô	Mathematics ◉ ◉	Science ◐ ◐	Art ⌄⌄ ⌄⌄
EARS Favorite Sport	Baseball ᖯ ᗷ	Football ◠ ◠	Soccer ᖳ ᗷ	Tennis d b
NOSE Favorite Weekend Activity	∠ Movies	○ Playing	⌣ Sports	↙ Reading
MOUTH Number of People in Your Family	Two ⏝	Three	Four	Five	Six or More

Data Analysis and Probability

Anika and Tyrone asked 30 people what kind of ice cream they liked the best out of 5 choices. The results are below.

1 Four people like black cherry.

2 Half as many people like mint chocolate as like black cherry.

3 The number of people who like strawberry is equal to mint chocolate and black cherry together.

4 The number of people who like chocolate is equal to strawberry and black cherry together.

5 The rest like vanilla.

The category that has the greatest number is called the *mode*. What flavor is the mode?

Number and Operations

What is the mystery number?
I am 1 more than the product of 2 consecutive even numbers greater than 4 but less than 12, the sum of which creates my inverse. What am I?

Data Analysis and Probability

You are one of 1,000 people who have entered the WEAR radio sweepstakes. Half of the people who entered will be selected to participate in the final drawing. Five of the entries in the final drawing will win a free trip; 4 will go to Mexico; and 1 person will win an all-expense-paid trip around the world. What is the probability, when you first drop it in the box, that your entry will win the trip around the world? Suppose that your entry was in the half selected for the final drawing. Now what is the probability that your entry will win the trip around the world? Believe it or not, your entry is one of the 5 selected for the free trip. Now what is the probability that you will win the trip around the world?

Geometry

Draw lines to connect every pair of dots below.
Count the number of lines drawn.
Name the polygons in the figures drawn.

Algebra

Write the following word expressions as numerical equations with variables.

a 5 less than a number

b 6 times a number plus 7 times the number

c the product of 9 and a number, decreased by 7

Number and Operations

The fifth grade science class is planning a class garden. The plot of land is 4 m wide and 5 m long. The chart shows how the class wants to divide the plot. Draw the garden and show the fractional parts.

Garden Area in Twentieths

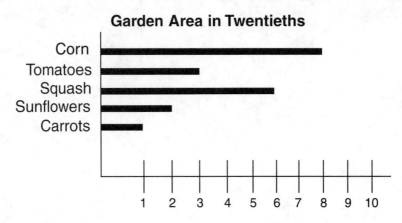

Problem Solving

Five of these pictures are of the same cube. Which one of the following is not a picture of the same cube?

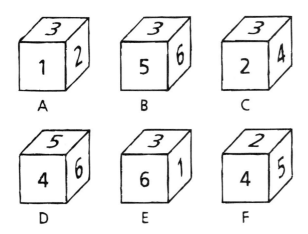

A   B   C

D   E   F

Number and Operations

What's the mystery number?

I am a 2-digit palindrome.

The sum of my digits is $\frac{1}{3}$ of the product of my digits.

What am I?

Measurement

Keisha has a carrying case for her tapes. The case is 25 cm long, 20 cm wide, and 8 cm deep. Each tape is 10 cm long, 6.5 cm wide, and 1.5 cm high. Draw a picture that shows a top view of the tapes, the view Keisha sees when she opens the lid. How many tapes does your picture show? Compare your answer with a partner's.

Algebra

The figure below is made up of 16 toothpicks. Take away 4 of the 16 toothpicks to make 4 equal triangles. Use real toothpicks to help you solve the problem.

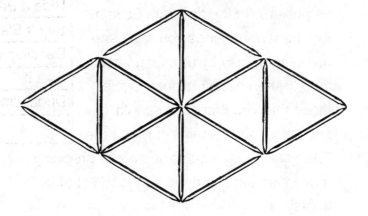

Algebra

A pair of standard dice is rolled so that a sum of 11 appears on top. What sum would be shown on the bottom of this pair? Use a set of dice to help you.

Number and Operations

Monica Morningside, the morning DJ for radio station WEAR, has 15 minutes left before her show ends. She wants to play as many of the songs shown as possible in the time left. Estimate the number of songs you think she has time to play by rounding each time to the nearest minute. Circle those that you think she should choose for the remaining 15 minutes. Then use a calculator to compute precisely how much total time the songs will take to play.

| | m = minute | s = second |
Song	Length
Ride a Bike with Me	3m 27s
Say It Sister	4m 04s
Dancing in the Park	3m 59s
Spill It	5m 00s
Dude, I'm Happy	4m 17s

Algebra

The fifth grade has a problem—someone is intercepting notes passed between friends. To solve the problem, some of the kids have been building secret codes. One code is shown below. Look for a pattern and then complete the secret code. After you complete the code, write a message to a friend. Ask your friend to decode it.

A	B	C	D	E	F	G	H	I	J	K	L	M
45	2	4	6	43	8	10	12	41				

N	O	P	Q	R	S	T	U	V	W	X	Y	Z

Measurement

There are 4 pecks in a bushel. A man sells tomatoes at $1.00 per bushel or $0.30 per peck. How much money will a customer save if he buys 100 bushels instead of 400 pecks?

Number and Operations

Each year 16,000 new icebergs form in the Arctic. Ninety percent of them can be found off the coast of Greenland where they pose no danger, unless they float into the open seas (about 400 of these icebergs do reach open waters). What fraction of the Arctic icebergs can be found off the coast of Greenland? What percentage of all Artic icebergs poses a problem? How could an iceberg in the open sea cause a problem for anyone?

Algebra

Find at least 5 sets of whole numbers that can be substitutes for x, y, and z in this equation. You can use the same number more than once (in different combinations of whole numbers).

$4x + 3y = 2z$

X	Y	Z

Algebra

This mystery number is not a multiple of 4.
It is an odd number.
It is not a multiple of 7.
It is not a multiple of 9.
The sum of its digits is less than 10.
It is not a multiple of 3.
The sum of its digits is 2.
The mystery number is _____ .

Number and Operations

The Stanislaski twins went out for pizza with 8 other friends. By mistake the pizza was cut into eighths.
Suggest ways the twins and their 8 friends can share the pizza. Can you give everyone equal size pieces? What if some agree to eat a smaller piece? On another paper, draw a picture to show your way of sharing the pizza. Explain why you used that way.

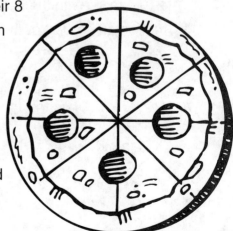

Number and Operations

Guess this number. Begin with the number of digits in a local telephone number (without the area code). Multiply that number by the number of s's in Mississippi. Now divide that number by the number of i's in that same river. Add the number of feet in a mile and subtract the temperature (in Fahrenheit) at which water freezes. What is the number? Make up another number-guessing problem. Have a friend solve your problem.

Algebra

Look at the set of numbers below. They are not in any particular order. Find something they have in common. Write a rule to go with the set of numbers. List 5 more numbers that could be part of the set.

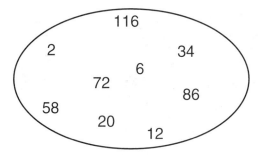

Rule:

Five other numbers:

Geometry

Which 3-dimensional shapes fit the clues below?
Write the letter of the shape

Only 1 of my faces is a circle.
I have a curved surface.
What shape am I? _____

I have 6 faces.
Each face is the same shape.
What shape am I? _____

Two of my faces are hexagons.
Six of my faces are rectangles.
What shape am I? _____

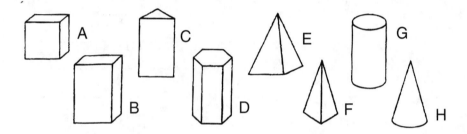

Algebra

The number of people in a football stadium doubles every 10 minutes. After an hour, the stadium is full. When was the stadium half full?

Algebra

Look at the function table. Find out the rule being used on the numbers going in. Complete the table.

Number in	Number out
11	26
8	23
35	50
3	18
55	70
7	
20	
2	
42	

Measurement

For the Art Fair, the students have been given permission to use the rectangular upper athletic field, which measures 200 yd. x 100 yd. If they must reserve 10,000 sq. ft. for aisles and fire exits, and each exhibit has 100 sq. ft. for its display, how many displays can be presented at the Art Fair?

Geometry

When Mrs. Peterson left the classroom last night she had the geometric solids all set for today's math class. The shapes looked like this:

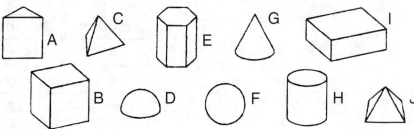

The janitor accidentally knocked the shapes below off the teacher's desk. Find which shapes fell off the desk. Write the letter of each shape so the janitor can put them where they belong.

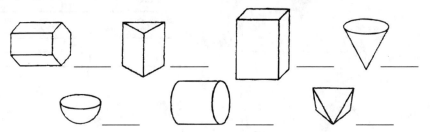

Number and Operations

How can you write four 9s so that together they equal 100?

Algebra

This Venn diagram has been completed except for the labels.
Look at what is in each region. Write an appropriate label in
each box.

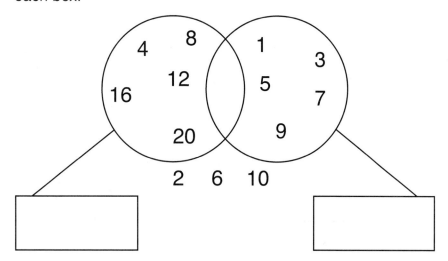

Measurement

A clock reads 10:45 A.M. when the power goes off for 1 hour
and 53 minutes. To what time should the clock be reset?

71

Algebra

Look at the pyramid. What numbers should be placed inside the two squares? How do you know? **Note:** don't use the number 1.

$$
\begin{array}{ccccccccc}
 & & & & 48 & & & & \\
 & & & 6 & & 8 & & & \\
 & & 2 & & 3 & & 8 & & \\
 & 2 & & 3 & & 4 & & 2 & \\
2 & & \square & & 2 & & \square & & 2 \\
\end{array}
$$

Problem Solving

My mother is 6 times older than my sister.
My sister is 36 years younger than my father.
My father is 3 times my age.
If my sister is 6, how old am I?

Number and Operations

At the Surfs-Up Water Park there are two hotels: Wave Runner and Beach Side. Use the clues below to decide how many guests are staying at each hotel.

 a Seventeen rooms cannot be used because they are being remodeled. Each floor of Wave Runner has 13 rooms. An average of 4 guests are staying in each room. Wave Runner had 34 floors. _____ people are staying at Wave Runner.

 b Beach Side has 20 floors. On even-numbered floors there are 17 rooms. An average of 3 guests are staying in each room. On odd-numbered floors there are 27 rooms. _____ people are staying at Beach Side.

Problem Solving

What number should replace the * on this view of the same dice?

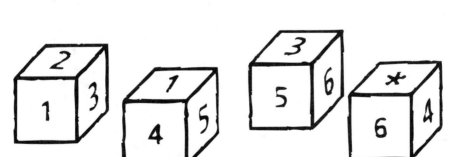

Data Analysis and Probability

Neema is making a picnic lunch for her friends. The choices for sandwiches are turkey, ham, or cheese. The choices for drinks are lemonade and juice.

Neema made a tree diagram to help organize her choices.
Fill in the missing lunches in the tree diagram.
How many different lunches are possible?

```
              ┌─── turkey  _____   lemonade and turkey
lemonade ─────┼─── ham     _____   _____
              └─── cheese  _____   _____

              ┌─── turkey  _____   _____
juice    ─────┼─── ham     _____   _____
              └─── cheese  _____   _____
```

Algebra

If $a \times b = 24$ and $b \times 5 = 15$, then what numbers do a and b represent?

0-7424-1795-6 Daily Warmups

Problem Solving

Use the chart and the clues below to find out who the midnight to 6 A.M. D.J. is on this week's work schedule.

	6 A.M. to noon	Noon to 6 P.M.	6 P.M. to midnight	Midnight to 6 A.M.
KT				
Bouncing Bob				
Mr. Smith				
Shadow Man				

1 KT can meet a friend for lunch at 1:00 P.M.

2 Mr. Smith does not start or finish his show at midnight.

3 The Shadow Man is asleep in bed from 1:00 A.M. until 10:00 A.M.

4 Bouncing Bob is responsible for the 8:00 A.M. traffic report during his show.

Algebra

Complete this pattern:

A	50	Z	1	B	49	Y	2											

Measurement

Carlos and Juana have come to a sign on the trail. On another paper, draw the trail. Draw the sign, falls, bridge, and cabin on the trail. Create a scale and fit your drawing on one piece of paper.

Algebra

The beginning of the Fibonacci sequence of numbers looks like this: 1, 1, 2, 3, 5, 8, 13, . . .

Circle each number below that fits within the Fibonacci sequence.

150

987

601

1,597

55

375

Algebra

Mr. De Jager, the postman, never likes to take the same route twice. However, he also hates to backtrack. How many different routes can you design for him? Routes can go forward or move to the side but can never go backward.

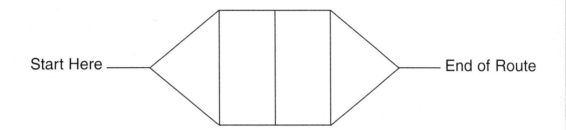

Start Here ——— End of Route

Number and Operations

The difference between 2 numbers is 5. Their product is 36. What are the 2 numbers?

Geometry

Draw 2 lines across the hexagon to divide it into the shapes listed.

1 triangle

2 four-siders

1 five-sider

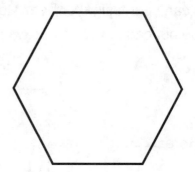

Algebra

Use a calculator and a number line.

The Wahmhoff twins are pouring water from the bathtub onto the floor at the rate of 2 gallons every minute. Renee is soaking up the water on the floor and pouring it down the sink at a rate of 1 gallon every minute. If the bathtub was filled with 10 gallons of water when all this began, how much time will have passed before Renee cleans up the last of the water? How much water will she have cleaned up at the end of 5 minutes? How much will she have cleaned up at the end of 6 minutes?

Problem Solving

Fiona just built this dartboard. How many different ways can you score exactly 100 points by throwing just 4 darts, assuming that all of your throws stick to the board?

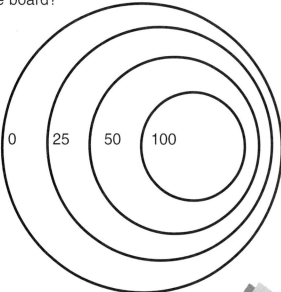

0   25   50   100

Algebra

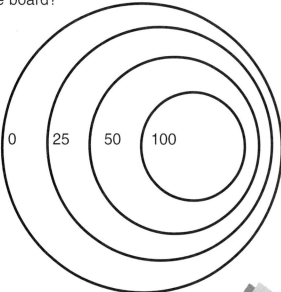

Take a number that is 4 times as large as another number. Use these 2 numbers to determine whether the following statement is true or false: If you add 20 to the smaller of the 2 numbers, that number will be only 6 less than the larger number. Provide 3 examples to show how this is true or false.

0-7424-1795-6 *Daily Warmups*

Number and Operations

The fifth grade at West Middle School puts out the school's weekly newspaper. Each paper contains 3,500 words, spread evenly across 4 pages. Each week four students are assigned to enter the text into the computer. This week, Annan, who types 20 words per minute, will enter the text for page 1. Margarid, who types 28 words per minute, will enter the text for page 2. Alex, who types 17 words per minute, will enter the text for page 3. Hua, who types 15 words per minute, will enter the text for page 4. Find the order in which the students will finish typing and how long it will take each one (round their times to the nearest minute). Place their names in this sentence so that it is true.

_____ > _____ < _____ > _____

Data Analysis and Probability

Professor Pompous has forgotten the combination to his safe, which has 2 dials. The left dial has numbers from 1 to 6, and the right dial has numbers from 1 to 4. What is the probability that Professor Pompous will get the correct combination the first time if he has no idea what the combination is?

Problem Solving

What's wrong with this picture? This may appear to be a normal street scene to you, but there are many mathematical errors taking place. How many of them can you find?

Data Analysis and Probability

Shalti is painting a toy box for his little sister. He is using 2 different colors: 1 for the inside of the box, and 1 for the outside of the box. He has this choice of colors for the outside: white, blue, and green. He has these choices for the inside: yellow, green, blue, and red. What are the possible combinations of colors that he can use?

Algebra

Connect each set of dots below so that every dot has a line drawn from it to each of the other dots. Record the number of lines drawn in the table.

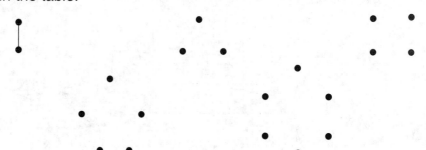

Number of dots	2	3	4	5	6
Number of lines	1				

Problem Solving

In a recent gymnastics meet, Rachel scored 21 points more than Carrie, who scored 7 fewer than Nani. Do you have enough information to determine how many points Nani scored? If so, what is her score? If not, what's missing?

0-7424-1795-6 *Daily Warmups*

Algebra

In a magic square, the sum of each row, column, and diagonal is the same. Use the clues to fill in the missing numbers for this square.

	7		
		15	
9			6

Clues:

- Numbers 6–21 are used in the squares.
- The sum of each row, column, and 4-number diagonal is 54.
- Each row, column, and diagonal has 2 even numbers.
- The first and last numbers in the first 2 columns are odd.
- The first and last numbers in the last 2 columns are even.

Geometry

Read the shape riddle and draw the answer.

I have 3 sides.

All 3 sides intersect.

Two lines are perpendicular.

What am I?

Number and Operations

After a day at the amusement park, Joel's class had a half hour before their bus departed. Five-tenths of the students went back for a ride on the carousel. Five-tenths of the others went for a ride on the Ferris wheel. Five-tenths of the remaining students went to get an ice cream. The remaining 5 students waited on benches for the bus. How many students were there in all?

Algebra

The Digit Distorter uses 2 different rules to change a number. When a number goes in, the first rule changes the number and a different number comes out. The Digit Distorter puts that number in again but uses a different rule to make a new number come out. Look at the numbers in the table. Find the rules used to change each number. Use the rules to complete the table.

IN	4	6	8	5	10	12
OUT	8	12				
IN	8	12				
OUT	10	14				

Rule 1:

Rule 2:

Geometry

Which 3-dimensional shapes fit the clues below?
Write the letter of the shape.

I have 4 faces.
All of my faces are triangles.
None of my faces are rectangles.
What shape am I? _____

I have 1 face.
If you push me I will roll.
What shape am I? _____

I have 6 faces.
None of my faces are square.
All of my faces are rectangles.
What shape am I? _____

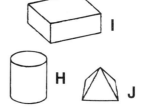

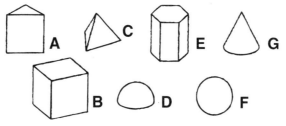

Number and Operations

Which is greater, 25% of 80 or 20% of 90?

Algebra

Aunt Agatha likes only certain numbers. Today she likes 18, 24, 15, 57, 36, and 60. She doesn't like 6, 22, 31, 40, and 102. Name 3 more numbers Aunt Agatha likes today.

Number and Operations

What is the Roman numeral for 769?

Algebra

Find the answer for the equation below given the change in the variable.

$$a + 59 = b$$

a	b
20	
103	
98	

Number and Operations

Jill and Nga are making a video history of the downtown area. They plan to tape 30 minutes of live action themselves. A local museum has agreed to provide them with twice as much historical film as the live action they plan to shoot. Then, the city commissioner gave them a video of the future vision for the city. This video runs $\frac{3}{4}$ the length of the museum film. How long will the presentation be when they have put all of the pieces together? Use your calculator to convert estimated times to exact hours and minutes.

165

Number and Operations

If odd numbers are kumquats and even numbers are oranges,

 a what is a kumquat plus a kumquat?

 b what is an orange plus an orange?

 c what is an orange plus a kumquat?

166

Algebra

Cary is on the track team. Angella is on the softball team. They like to walk home together on days when they both have practice. Cary has practice every other day, and Angella has practice every third day. They both have practice on March 1. How often will they walk home together in March? On which dates will they walk together?

Number and Operations

June has this money in her purse: 15 dimes, 10 quarters, 5 one-dollar bills, 2 five-dollar bills, and 1 ten-dollar bill. She goes to the store and buys a compact disk. With tax, the disk costs $17.75. June wants to pay the exact amount and use the fewest bills and coins she can? Make a chart that shows which and how many coins and bills she should use. Prove that these coins and bills add up to $17.75.

Geometry

Draw as many straight lines as listed to divide the triangle into the shapes listed.

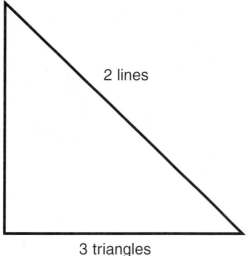

2 lines

3 triangles

Measurement

Angela helps coach Pee Wee soccer. For each practice, she brings 5 packages of Wowee Punch mix and water to the soccer field. The package directions for the drink call for 1 package of mix and 10 times that much water. One package of drink mix is 12 oz. Each day, the soccer players splash 20% of the water on their faces to cool down. All of the remaining water is used in preparing the Wowee Punch. There are 128 oz. in a gallon. How many gallons of water are available for face splashing? Round your answer to the nearest whole number.

Number and Operations

The measure of this rectangle is one whole.
Name the fractional part, decimal equivalent, and percent represented shown by each type of square.

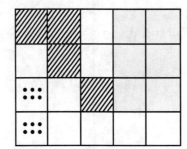

Algebra

Two factory workers, Burly and Curly, each work at different speeds on different shifts. Burly works a 6-hour shift and makes 12 parts per hour. Curly works an 8-hour shift and makes 10 parts per hour.

a In 1 shift, which worker makes more parts?

b In 1 shift, how many parts do the 2 workers make altogether?

c In 24 hours of work time, how many parts do the 2 workers make altogether?

Number and Operations

Rosa painted $\frac{1}{4}$ of a canvas that is 3 ft. x 4 ft. Emily painted $\frac{1}{2}$ of a canvas that is 1 ft. x 3 ft. Which statement is true?

a Rosa painted half again as much as Emily.

b Rosa painted twice as much as Emily.

c Emily painted half again as much as Rosa.

d Emily painted twice as much as Rosa.

Number and Operations

Giselle wants to buy some envelopes for letters she is writing. At the store the sign on the envelopes says they are sold at the rate of 4 for $0.21 (including sales tax). Giselle has $1.00. What is the greatest number of envelopes she can buy? In the space below, write and draw to explain how you reached your answer.

Measurement

While their mother was speaking on the telephone, the Walker twins emptied the contents of a 5-lb. bag of flour on the floor and covered it with 8 oz. of honey, 24 oz. of cola, and 2 pt. of cream. Then they emptied a 36-oz. bag of granola, a 60-oz. bag of yeast, $\frac{1}{4}$ lb. of baking soda, and 12 oz. of vinegar over the mess. Make 2 lists: one for the dry materials and the other for the liquids. Find the total weight of the dry materials and the total volume of the liquid materials.

Measurement

Holey Hole! Miners, searching for the world's largest diamonds, managed to dig the world's biggest hole. Using only wheelbarrows, picks, and shovels, they removed 25,300,000 tons of dirt. Find out how many wheelbarrows filled with dirt the miners carried to the edge of the mine, if each wheelbarrow held an average of 50 lb. of dirt. If a diamond was found weighing 1% of the total weight of the dirt from the wheelbarrows, how much did the diamond weigh in tons?

Algebra

The students at Washington Elementary School held a car wash to earn money for assemblies. They charged $2.00 for each car. The first hour they washed 5 cars. The second hour they washed 7 cars. The third hour they washed 9 cars. Every hour, they washed 2 more cars than the hour before. At this rate how long did it take them to wash 100 cars altogether? If they needed to earn $500.00, how long would they need to wash cars?

Geometry

Name the shape.

I have 4 sides. One pair of sides is parallel. The other pair of sides would intersect if they were extended.

What am I? _____

Data Analysis and Probability

Alan, Ian, and Duncan were judges for the annual third-grade art show. Each was asked to pick 3 winners. Alan picked Thao, Kessie, and Hana. Ian picked Mary, Hana, and Seb. Duncan picked Thao, Seb, and Hana. Create a Venn diagram that shows which entrants were picked by the 3 judges.

Algebra

Regan's grandfather gave her 2 guesses to tell him what coins he had in his pocket. If she guessed correctly, she would get to keep all the money. Grandpa gave her these clues:

- There are 4 times as many quarters as half-dollars.
- There are fewer than 12 quarters.
- There are fewer than 8 dimes.
- There are twice as many nickels as dimes.
- The total value of the coins is $4.00.

How many of each coin is in Grandpa's pocket?

Geometry

On the grid below draw a net for the rectangular prism shown.
Calculate its surface area and perimeter.

Perimeter:

Area: **Net:**

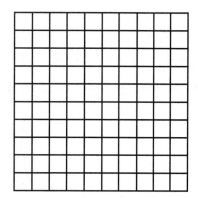

Number and Operations

Dave wants to make a wood sign. One piece of wood is $\frac{2}{6}$ of a foot and the other is $\frac{3}{8}$ of a foot long. If Dave combines these 2 pieces, will the sign be longer than $\frac{1}{2}$ foot? $\frac{3}{4}$ foot? Name a fraction piece that, if Dave had it, would allow him to show this combination exactly.

Measurement

The Walker twins have discovered rolls: rolls of toilet tissue, rolls of paper towels, and even rolls of aluminum foil. One evening the twins managed to unroll every roll of a 12-pack of toilet tissue (280 sheets, each sheet is 4.4 in. long), 4 rolls of paper towels (100 sheets, each sheet is 6.5 in. long), and three 104-ft. rolls of aluminum foil. Danny, who was unlucky enough to be baby-sitting this evening, was able to re-roll only 2 ft. for every 3 ft. the twins unrolled. How many feet did Danny re-roll? In figuring out your answers, round all numbers to the nearest foot.

Algebra

Overdue library fines at one library are $0.10 per day per book and $0.05 per day per magazine. Polly just returned 3 books and 3 magazines that were 1 week late. How much does she owe the library?

Number and Operations

This number has a 0 in the ones place. The fifth digit to the right of the decimal sign is less than the first. The number in the thousandths place is the smallest number. The number in the ten-thousandths place is half the value of the number in the hundreds place. This decimal contains a 4, 2, 1, 3, and 5. What is the number?

Number and Operations

Aunt Agatha likes only certain numbers. She likes 2, 5, 7, 23, and 31. She doesn't like 4, 6, 21, and 30. Name 3 more numbers that Aunt Agatha likes.

Algebra

Pets R Us is having an ugly dog contest to raise money for the local animal shelter. A hairless dog named Harry, a mongrel named Max, and a mixed-breed named Peaches entered the contest. The dog with the most points is the winner. Together Harry and Max have 44 points. Harry and Peaches together have 56 points. Max and Peaches together have 48 points. Who is the ugliest dog?

Number and Operations

Christian is stocking up on supplies for his two-week camping trip and has $15.00 to spend. He wants to buy 2 stuff sacks ($3.50 each), 1 bottle of super bug spray ($1.15), 2 candy bars ($0.39 each), and 1 pack of action comics ($4.59). Estimate whether he has enough money to buy all of the items he wants. Then, using your calculator, compute the total cost of these items plus an 8% sales tax (round your answers to the nearest cent). How much money will he have left over (or how much will he be short)?

Algebra

The kids living around the school love to play basketball on Saturdays. They have won 5 games in a row against their parents. Amazingly, they won each game with a score just 1 point higher than the previous game. If they scored a total of 515 points in the 5-game series, what were the kids' scores for each game?

Algebra

At the pet shop Marin and Dan bought a lizard, along with 36 crickets for him to eat. The first day they had him, the lizard didn't eat any crickets. He was probably nervous in his new home. The second day he ate 1 cricket. The third day he ate 2 crickets. The fourth day he ate 3 crickets. If he continues to eat at this rate, how long will it be before he has eaten all the crickets?

Number and Operations

Rachel and Faizah are trying to set the price of candy in the school store. Rachel says that they will make the most money if they sell 4 gumballs for $0.11 each. Faizah says that they should sell 6 gumballs for $0.21 each. Which price would be the best for the customers? Which price would be the best for the store?

Measurement

A string of holiday lights is 8 ft. long and has a bulb every 4 in. What is the maximum number of lights on this string?

Number and Operations

In one 24-hour day, Kevin spends $\frac{1}{3}$ of his time asleep, $\frac{1}{4}$ of his time in school, and $\frac{1}{12}$ of his time doing homework. How many hours does Kevin have free for everything else?

193

Number and Operations

Huong, Josef, and Devon are taking part in the annual walk to raise funds for the homeless. Each of them collected pledges in support of each mile they walked, and all 3 of them completed the 15-mile walk-a-thon. Huong collected pledges totaling $3.50 per mile, Josef had $\frac{2}{3}$ of Huong's pledge amount, and Devon had 0.75 of Josef's pledge amount. What was the total amount collected by each walker? Round your answers to the nearest cent.

194

Algebra

Solve the fruit salad problem. Write the number of each kind of fruit.

There are 15 pieces of fruit.

Oranges make up $\frac{1}{5}$ of the salad.

There are an equal number of apples and bananas.

Apples = _____

Bananas = _____

Oranges = _____

Measurement

Which package holds more?

Package A: 4 in. x 5 in. x 5 in.

Package B: 8 in. x 6 in. x 2 in.

Number and Operations

Ehab lives near a community garden. The whole garden is 60 ft. x 100 ft. Ehab's family tends $\frac{1}{6}$ of the total area. Draw the community garden and show the area of the garden Ehab's family tends.

Number and Operations

What is the base-ten number for this Roman numeral?

MMMCDLIX

Measurement

The distance from the base of Yodel Mountain to its peak is 15,840 vertical feet. If you plan to walk to the top, however, you will have to follow a trail that is 6 times longer than the vertical distance. How many miles long is the trail?

0-7424-1795-6 *Daily Warmups*

Number and Operations

Elizabeth and her sister have been collecting coins for the last 5 years. They now have a collection of 5,236 pennies, nickels, and dimes, and have decided to sort all of their coins. If it took them 15 minutes to sort 169 coins, estimate (by rounding) how long it will take them to sort the entire collection. Use a calculator to confirm your estimate.

Measurement

How many 6-in. pieces of rope can be cut from a mile-long rope?

Problem Solving

Use play coins to help you. Colleen's father always lets her keep the change she finds stuck between the cushions in the couch. Last week she found 10 coins worth $1.19. Her father wanted to exchange the coins for a $1.00 bill, but Colleen couldn't give him exactly $1.00 in change. One of the coins was a half dollar (which Colleen wouldn't trade anyway, since she collects them). What were the other 9 coins? Now use coins to write 2 of your own coin puzzlers.

Number and Operations

Two hundred seventy-five students showed up for the annual school clean up on Saturday. The fifth grade collected $6\frac{4}{5}$ bags of trash. The sixth grade collected $1\frac{1}{4}$ as many bags as the fifth grade. The seventh and eighth grades tied, with $\frac{6}{8}$ the number of bags collected by the sixth grade. What is the total number of bags of trash collected by the students?

Data Analysis and Probability

The high temperature one winter day in Marquette, Michigan, was −20°F. The next day it was 0°F, and on the third day it was 14°F. What was the average temperature in Marquette for those 3 days?

Number and Operations

Solve this problem. Start at the end and work backward. Lizzy and a group of her friends went to a casting event for a TV commercial. Half of the group was too nervous to try out. Of the remaining half, $\frac{2}{3}$ couldn't return on the filming day. Of those remaining, $\frac{1}{2}$ flubbed the TV audition. The one remaining student was Lizzy. She got the part! How many were in Lizzy's group of friends at the start?

Algebra

Berta's Burrito Barn uses a special machine to prepare burritos. When Berta enters a number in the burrito machine, a different number of burritos come out. First she entered 5, and 12 burritos came out. Next she punched in 9, and out came 24 burritos. Then she entered 12, and 33 burritos popped out. What rule is the burrito machine using? How many burritos will come out if she enters 15?

Number and Operations

Use dice to help you solve.

A set of 2 standard dice is rolled so that the sum of the numbers on top is 10. What is the sum of the numbers shown on the bottom of these 2 dice?

Algebra

Find the answer for the equation below given the change in the variable.

$$48 \div x = y$$

x	y
4	
8	
6	

Number and Operations

Solve these by inserting operation marks (+, −, x, ÷) and parentheses.

3 2 4 2 = 0

8 8 32 4 = 8

Number and Operations

Suppose that 4 people in your family each take 5 showers a week, and that each shower lasts for 10 minutes. If your shower uses 6 gallons of water per minute, how many gallons of water does your family use for showers in 1 week?

Measurement

Arlene works at the Candy Counter. Yesterday she sold 5 boxes of chocolate that each weighed $\frac{1}{2}$ lb. and 4 boxes of licorice that each weighed $\frac{3}{4}$ lb. How many pounds of candy did Arlene sell in all?

Problem Solving

Arrange these students in order from youngest to oldest.
Mary is older than Jason, who is younger than Randi, who would be
equal in age to Lan Ho if Lan Ho were 3 years older. However, Lan
Ho is still 2 years younger than Greg, whose friend, Lori, was born
just 4 days after Mary and 4 days before Randi.

Number and Operations

On a trip to Yellowstone National Park, Brigit discovers that
her family travels about 41 mi. in 45 minutes. If the family
travels at this rate for 6 hours, how far do they go? Explain
what your answer is and why you believe it is correct.

Number and Operations

Troy says, "I have $0.65. I have fewer nickels than pennies, fewer dimes than nickels, fewer quarters than dimes." In the space below, solve the riddle by making a chart that shows a combination of coins equal to $0.65.

Geometry

Consider a tennis ball can that holds 3 tennis balls.

Does the height of the can appear to be greater

or less than the distance around the can?

If a tennis ball has a diameter of 2.5 in., the

height of the can is at least _____ .

The distance around the can is at least _____.

215

Algebra

In each problem below, the answer is given. Write an appropriate question. Jamie left at 1:00 P.M. with a full tank of gas. After driving 165 mi., she stopped at 4:00 P.M. and bought $9.24 worth of gas, which filled the tank. The gas cost $1.40 a gallon.

1. If the answer is *55 mph*, what is the question?
2. If the answer is *the amount of gas*, what is the question?
3. If the answer is *25 mpg*, what is the question?

216

Number and Operations

Here's a challenge for you. You have five seconds to write the largest number you can. There are just two rules.

1. You cannot use the same numeral twice.
2. You cannot place 2 consecutive numerals next to each other.

Work with a partner. When you're done, square the number and label all of the units—tens, hundreds, thousands, and so on—until you've labeled every place value in your new number.

Number and Operations

Mary has $1.00 to spend at the candy store. Lollipops are $0.25 each, chocolates are $0.10 each, and toffees are $0.05 each. If Mary buys 2 lollipops, how many toffees can she buy?

Algebra

The fifth graders are collecting cans of food. They collected twice as many cans on Tuesday as they did on Monday, which was only $\frac{1}{4}$ the number they collected on Thursday. If they collected 20 cans on Friday and this was an increase of 4 over their collection the day before, how many cans of food did they collect in all over the 4 days?

Number and Operations

Hannah's hash contains 3 parts beef for every 4 parts potato. If Hannah wants to make a total of 21 lb. of hash, how many pounds of meat and potatoes does she need?

Measurement

The Hales have decided to get a puppy. First they must put up a chain link fence in the front yard, the side yard, and the back yard. Each of these fences was to be rectangular, with a post at every corner and then spaced every 6 ft. along the fence. Unfortunately, their twins managed to pull up 50% of the fence posts before the fencing could be attached. Find the perimeter of each fence. Determine how many fence posts there were originally and how many the twins dug up.

Front yard: length = 24 ft., width = 48 ft.

Back yard: length = 18 ft., width = 18 ft.

Side yard: length = 42 ft., width = 12 ft.

Algebra

The carpet on your floor is twice as long as it is wide and the total area of your room is less than 50 sq. ft. What are the possible dimensions of your carpet? Write a statement using 2 variables and the symbol < to show how you can find the possible answers. Then find at least 2.

Number and Operations

Dan and Sara's mom made chocolate chip cookies. Dan took $\frac{3}{6}$ of the cookies for his baseball team. Sara sneaked $\frac{2}{16}$ of Dan's cookies for her friends. What fraction of his original amount of cookies does Dan have left?

Algebra

Alex, Baxter, and Conner had a contest to see who could jog the most miles in a month. Together Alex and Baxter jogged 21 miles. The combined total for Alex and Conner was 19. Together Conner and Baxter ran 22 miles. Who ran the farthest?

Number and Operations

Fran has 100 animals. She has 25 chickens, 15 cows, and the rest are sheep. What fraction tells how many of her animals are sheep? Reduce your answer to lowest terms.

Number and Operations

During a period of 1 year, 2,000,000 special-edition duck stamps were sold in the United States at $1.00 a stamp. The money was used to preserve wetlands. How many acres of wetlands would be saved from the proceeds at a cost of $1,200.00 an acre? Round your answer to the nearest dollar.

Algebra

The Smith family owns 2 cars, 4 bicycles, 1 unicycle, and 2 tricycles. How many tires are there in all?

Number and Operations

Lisa and Pete shared a small apple pie. Lisa ate more than $\frac{1}{2}$ but less than $\frac{3}{4}$. Pete ate more than $\frac{1}{4}$ but less than $\frac{1}{2}$. What part of the pie did each of them eat?

Lisa ate _____.

Pete ate _____.

Algebra

Radio station WEAR is holding one of its annual listener contests. To win a caller must be able to complete this pattern. Anyone who does complete it will win the dollar amount equal to the last number in the series. How much will they win?

3, 9, 81, 4, 16, 256, _____, _____, _____

Algebra

This year I am 4 times as old as my daughter. In 20 years, I will be twice as old as my daughter. What are our ages this year?

Number and Operations

Amber scored 20 points in last night's basketball game. If she made 3 free throws and 3 three-pointers, how many 2-point baskets did she make?

0-7424-1795-6 *Daily Warmups*

Number and Operations

How many legs would there be…

 a in a crowd of 300 bipeds?

 b in a herd of 300 quadrupeds?

 c in a group of 300 centipedes?

Data Analysis and Probability

Nick and his friends built a miniature race car using an old lawn mower engine and spare parts they picked up at Recycled Auto Parts. They had a budget of $100.00. Create a pie graph that shows how their money was spent.

Engine	$25.00
Wheels	$2.50 each
Frame materials	$50.00
Fuels and lubricants	$5.00
Paint	$10.00

Algebra

I have 5 brothers. Each of my brothers has 1 sister. How many children are in my family?

Number and Operations

What's wrong with this problem?

The Orens, a family of 5, ordered a pizza to eat while watching a movie on Friday night. Each one of them ate $\frac{2}{3}$ of the 18-slice pizza. How many pieces did each member of the family eat?